Different caterpillars eat different types of food. In this story, Flora raises a monarch butterfly. Monarch caterpillars eat milkweed. If you are going to raise a butterfly, identify what it's eating and not just where it happens to be sitting. Avoid feeding gypsy moth and tent caterpillars. Use a caterpillar identification guide to learn more.

Flora's Caterpillar

Written by A.D. Anderson

Illustrated by Tricia Peterson

BLUERAVEN CREATIVE
ideas that fly

Blueraven Creative, LLC

Lake Barrington, IL

© 2018

This book is dedicated
to those who nurture the world
and others who will someday.

For Liam and Lance—A.A.
For Will Archer—T.P.

Flora loves butterflies!

Every summer she sees them
fluttering from flower to flower. She tries
to catch them, but they usually get away.
Oh, how Flora wishes she could have a butterfly!

One day, as she was looking at a milkweed plant
in her garden, she saw a caterpillar crawling along
the edge of a leaf. "Crunch, crunch, crunch,"
it chewed merrily with each tiny step.

Flora watched in wonder.

"I would love to see you turn into a butterfly,"
she said to the caterpillar, carefully placing
it into a large plastic box.

The caterpillar looked up.

"What are you doing, Flora?"
asked her mom.

"I'm going to watch a caterpillar become a
butterfly!" exclaimed Flora.

Mom gazed in the box at the small caterpillar.
"Do you know what kind of caterpillar this is?"
asked Mom.

"No, but I'll find out," said Flora.

Opening the lid of the box, Flora gently sprinkled grass around the caterpillar.

"I wonder why he's not moving," said Flora.

9

Caterpillar Identification

Gypsy Moth

Tomato Hornworm

Black Swallowtail

Monarch

Pulling out her tablet,

Flora opened a window and found pictures of caterpillars that turned into moths and butterflies.

Scrolling down the page, Flora found a caterpillar that looked just like the one in her box.

The caterpillar appeared to smile.

"Mom! Mom! I found it,"
exclaimed Flora. "It's a monarch caterpillar!"

Looking at the caterpillar in the box, then at
the one on the screen, Flora's mom agreed.
"Do you know what a monarch caterpillar eats?"

"Green leaves," said Flora, "because that's what
it shows in the picture."

Taking a closer look at the website with her mom,
Flora discovered monarchs eat milkweed.

So Flora took the caterpillar out of the box and tossed out the grass. Then she put in a clean paper towel, a fresh milkweed leaf, and a long twig.

Uninterested in the stick,

the caterpillar rapidly ate the leaf.

"What are those tiny black balls?" asked Flora, pointing at the bottom of the box.

"*Frass* is a word scientists use for poop that comes from insects," explained Mom.

The caterpillar climbed the stick.

Every day, Flora dumped the frass
in the garden and gave the caterpillar a
fresh milkweed leaf.

A week later, the caterpillar was as long
as Flora's thumb, but he was not interested
in the leaves she put in the box.

"Mom, why did the caterpillar stop eating?"
asked Flora.

"The caterpillar is getting ready
to change into a butterfly,"
said Mom.

Mom went with Flora to look at the caterpillar, which was now hanging upside down like a letter "J" from the little branch.

"It's dead," cried Flora, looking at the lifeless little caterpillar. Mom tried to reassure her that it was changing into a chrysalis, but Flora knew better.

The caterpillar rested upside down.

The caterpillar disappeared.

The next day, she awoke ready to
make a grave for her little friend
when she saw the caterpillar had
disappeared. A tiny green bag
with a halo of golden dots was
hanging in his place.

"Look," said Flora, pointing
to the tiny green bag.

"That's the chrysalis," said Mom.
"In about ten days, a monarch
butterfly will hatch and fly away."

Flora watched the chrysalis change each day. She wondered why it was turning black. Her mom explained that they were starting to see the monarch's black stripes.

Each day, the chrysalis became
clearer and clearer until one morning,
the chrysalis began to open.
Something black with white dots
was trying to escape from beneath
an orange wing.

The monarch began to emerge.

Flora and her mom watched

the butterfly *s-t-r-e-t-c-h*
its slender black antennae
and reach for the bottom
of its chrysalis with six
thread-like legs.

The butterfly's wet,
crumpled wings
slowly opened and
closed around an
oversized abdomen.
After several minutes,
the wings looked bigger
and smoother.

Flora looked at the butterfly, then
back at her tablet. Her butterfly did
not have pouches on its hind wings,
so "he" was actually a "she."

Monarch Butterfly
Hind wing close up

ᴸᴱ
min veins
Black pouches
on hind wings

FEMALE
• Thick veins
• No pouches

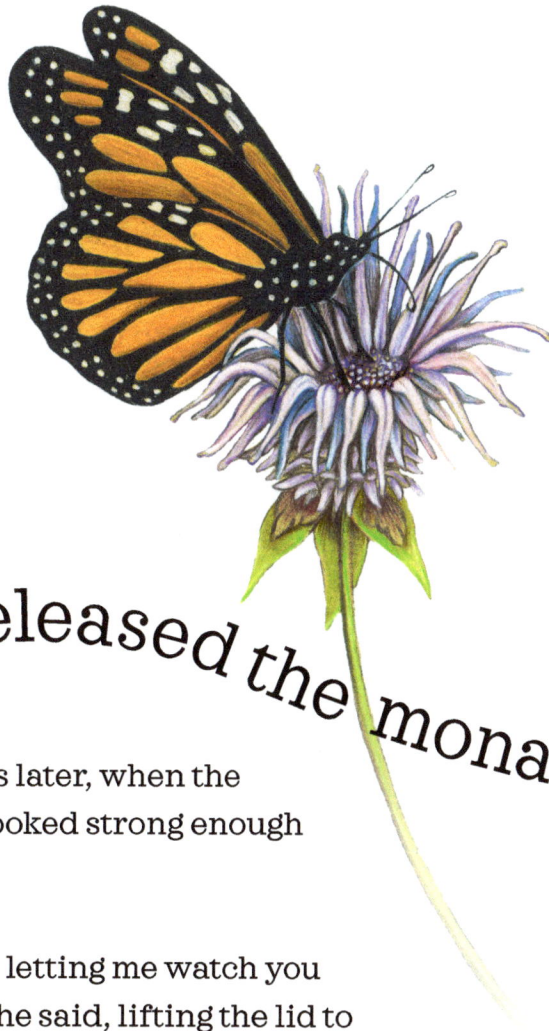

Flora released the monarch

a few hours later, when the butterfly looked strong enough to fly.

"Thanks for letting me watch you grow up," she said, lifting the lid to let the butterfly walk on her hand.

The butterfly opened her wings to bask in the warm sunlight, then fluttered to the garden to sip nectar from a fragrant bee balm plant. And Flora smiled.

To encourage butterflies to come
to your yard, provide food, water, and shelter.

- Butterflies need special plants to lay eggs
  and sip nectar. Native plants provide both.
  To learn more about native plants that can
  help butterflies where you live, contact your
  state's department of natural resources or
  local conservation group.
- Moist sand or mud provides a place
  for butterflies to sip water.
- Shrubs and trees shelter butterflies from
  predators and extreme weather.

www.ingramcontent.com/pod-product-compliance
Lightning Source LLC
Chambersburg PA
CBHW041245040426
42445CB00005B/146